Seeds of Light

By Amanda McGregor

All rights Reserved
Mookie Publishing
Amanda McGregor © Copyright
ISBN 978-0-9934881-9-1

Heartfelt and True

The doorway in to our hearts
Are often forgotten tales,
Keys left on the sideboard,
Unused and rusting at the edges.
We need to remember the value of enabling and opening such a magnificent doorway.
Through the gateway we see the palace that our hearts represent:
Our life, love and key to our future;
As we follow our hearts,
We find the pathway to complete our journey and arrive at our destiny.
Dare to take the key and look into your heart,
open the doorway,
What kind of palace or castle is inside?
Are the galleries filled with pictures of distant lands, lost loves, heartfelt truths?
Do the rooms feel light and airy?
Walking towards the centre, through a myriad of emotions,
What is the special tale that exists, so true to you?
Heartfelt and happy?
Or deceptive and painful?
Our souls remember the kindness and the sorrow of our past endurance.
To banish reconnecting to this story in our present lives,
We must search through the rooms,
Create peace and ask that those pained souls leave us.
Then invite angels and archangels to share our palace with light and joy.
Give a room to those people who are really special,
Whom you do really care about
and who have enough heart space themselves to really care for you,
We can look into our hearts desires,
By dreamily staring into the warm fire in the core of our palace,

Listening, as we look into the flames of the fire,
deep within,
Watching the flames dance;
Blue, purple, orange and white flickers.
The fire fairies speak to us,
reminding us of our desires;
We can ask them to create a vision of perfection,
A mansion filled with angels,
A love filled with ecstasy,
A journey filled with adventure and abundance.
Dare to dream of following your heart into the
deepest happiness
that your soul has ever known,
Allow the galleries to fill with visions of perfection,
Dare to fill your palace with an eternity of bliss,
heartfelt and true.
Peace be with you.

A Mirage of Love?

When Love is the depth of a river
How engulfed can we feel
Before choking on our true nature of circumstance?
When I was a girl my dreams were naive,
Innocent and wholesome.
Yet, having wandered from that path
I search through deep oceans to find that same
Pearl of choice,
In wisdom and purity,
The one true pearl for me.
The choices that present
Frequently do not attempt to capture
The innocence of my desires
As corrupted as I have become
I still want for this simplicity,
This pearl of choice
Desperate attempts to save my joy
Lead to a land of destitution
As I stand like a statue in the desert

Looking across the horizon at a crowd of chess pieces,
Fallen a long the way side
One true soul mate stands there, statuesque.
The wind howls between us,
We feel the brisk raw truth of our journey,
The velocity of our endeavors.
I loved him from that moment,
As I looked across the desert of fallen comrades,
Not one with the strength of their own conviction.
Yet the one true knight tarnished from his fight,
Stood strong fit and able to partner me
Like a walrus unravelling from the sea of life.

For Someone Special

When I lift the lid of the superficial world that surrounds us,
I look at your being as if you are absolute,
your energy surrounds me,
Positive to negative with a love that is thick,
Deep, enduring and wise.
Such a powerful love must be held in a shell of pith,
A nut to be opened.
From one day to the next you hold yourself in a mask of comedy,
Even though you understand the depths of a humans heart.
My heart opened to you when I felt your pain after a great loss,
It touched on something inside me,
An understanding of a familiar journey.
Before this time I didn't see or connect with the endurance of your life,
It was like a door that led me into the gravity of you
And gave me a vision of the content of your persona.
Seeing you as a three dimensional person,
I began to enter into an anxious chaos.

New to me, I was naïve, foolish and unrehearsed in dealing with such an intensity of emotions.
Caught up in my chaotic stutter,
Tripping over my innocence,
I plummeted towards a foolish awareness,
A need to take on the responsibilities of my own feelings and share a deep love,
Without questioning worth, time or approach.
I now find myself expressing a need to be close to you,
to live with a love straight from Heaven itself,
To build a life that is at home with angels and ecstasy.
A love that is not enduring, but wise and beautiful.
The light guides us to a place of serenity;
The depths will create a blessing to everyday I live.
I ridicule my own mask,
which represents a need to hold and protect my deep love,
For the first time, through you,
I see how superficial I am.

KISS ME

Give unto my soul a kiss deep enough to alleviate my eternal presence
Strong enough to take me to the highest pitch of light.
Don't ask me to beg
I ask out of innocence
Out of want
Out of honesty
With a passion to quench the thirst of my desires in fulfillment and wonder
At the Joy of Life.

Seeds of Light

The pain in my heart is like that of a droplet of light
fragmented into a thousand rays,
Stretching over the fields,
the light reaches out to the leaves on the trees.
The whispering woods know the nature of my pain,
far more than any human being.
Out of the night,
from my heart emerges a white light,
It moves away from my being.
Yes it is true,
My very own heart has had enough and it readily
flies away!
What comedy,
Even I do not desire this for myself.
Light on light weaves a thousand colours,
The fabric of the earth to be endured and enjoyed,
but also a net to catch all who fall into her darkness.
To sin, to some, is to be happy
To be true is to be dark,
such is the world we have created.
I must fly higher.

Burnt Out

Even now,
A heart burnt out,
Turned to coal,
still glistens in the morning sun,
Catching rays
Aimed in hope towards a turn in fortune.
To forget me not
Last night my heart was torched
by a man I allowed myself to love.
Following my heart into that pain made me question
the nature of my gain?

I was anticipating a different ending
to a story that was crushed so early on in the journey.
Whisper to me, for I am but a gasp away.

Shadows

Looking deeply through the muddy waters
I wonder what stirs beneath,
A monster in a lagoon of toxic interchange,
Thereafter the creature begins to awake from his slumber
Emerging through the sludge and slippery reeds,
As he approaches the surface he is met with the warmth of spring
Lily pads tightened their buds, waiting to perform to a glancing audience.
Deep breaths stir through the creature's gills,
He grasps at the grassland,
Saturated in dew on the banks
The freshness nourishes his empty malnourished stomach,
He pulls himself on to the water bank.
As he renews his passion,
sunning and still during lazy days.
We are met with the calmness of his heavy slumber
This creature brings peace to us in his splendour as he dwells.
One realises his freedom,
In abandonment of self-awareness
As he lies strong in the beauty of his magnificence.

Seeking, Through Me

Touching into the void of truth
I pass on understanding

Cutting through to the core
Of knowing,
Realising, having, dreaming,
Wanting and existing.
I need to be clear of my troubles
You need to be sure of yourself.
The world is a creative playground,
A myriad of emotions,
Held together with a core of love.
A pathway through a gateway,
The creation of a planet, a galaxy, a universe.
This is for you, this is your gift.
I am just here as a door keeper,
a guide,
A second sight.
Not wanting, just knowing and becoming.
Blessed are all those that seek to stand with me and fully 'become'.

The Spine of Existence

Central to our hopes and fears is a stone of granite
The stone is as much a part of us our past
We conquer it in madness
It is that which holds our integrity
Fundamental to the individual's needs
Is the spine of our humanity
The key to our inner peace and the tree of life that offers us complete understanding.
To be able to pick from this tree would mean that life is available for the taking;
We come to it kindly,
We ask from it humbly
We are given the fruits in abundance
The fruits are wise
They teach us as they are peeled
As they are tasted
As they are digested
Come back into the morrow land as I have another

thing to say;
It is not all for now
'There will be more trees bearing more fruits.

The Word

A task within our own reconciliation
We strive to show up to each other
In a true Light,
With seats of joy under our wings
Ready to embrace a new morning
Tenderly we touch our cheeks, to cheek,
Taking courage in our endeavors to assess our goals
And realise our intentions,
To create a perfect alliance
Without doubt or bereft of true meaning
We progress lightly on the foot
Deep in the heart
Dancing through the dewy moisture of our breath
Glancing through the depths of our desires
We find the connecting tissues of our souls, In that moment we cherish each other without want nor wish,
With an understanding deep enough to strike the darkest bow
And shoot ourselves into a life of ecstasy.

Phoenix

Carbon burnt
on my feathered quills
I seek a moment of tranquility
in an infinity of wonder,
Walking through the wall of fire
I breath in the flames of justice,
allowing my body to burn to dust.

Knowing, that with every breath,
I let go of my desires
my wants and needs
Ashes on the floor
ready to be swept away,
not to the river of kindness of which they belong,
to be swept under the carpet.
To ease peoples hearts
peoples minds
so they can accept their reality
to justify their happiness
To allow goodness in for all of us,
and for me;
I get the gift of eternity, of love and beauty
Light shines forth,
blinding all in my path.
A peace washes over me,
burning through the remnants of the past.
My breath shortens through this passage way
As I feel the vitality of life.
Freedom of a past vanquished to another.
I am given my new life
I breath freely,
Inspired by how much strength I am given to live
through my fate.

Give up the Game

Give up the Game
Give up the Game
Looking into the water,
The love you gave me was thwarted
My heart is looking for appeasement.
We whisper into hazes
And ask ourselves to remain.

I applaud you in your wisdom
For me it is a journey of reconciliation

A time for unnerving jubilation.
And now, a demand for a new game.

To be set free without the boundaries of a love
thwarted in its shadow
Don't be here for tomorrow,
Be ready for a new love.
A freedom will encounter
And bring us to the promised land
As its time to give up the game.

Embracing the Healing Forces of Nature

Thick mud energises and destroys me,
from one moment to the next.
I celebrate my integration with the earth,
Within a second I curse and weep.
My anger takes hold as I wish to be free from the
restraints
That hold me back.
I call out to the angels, 'Can you carry me?'
'Not this time' comes the reply.
'Can I disclaim?'
'Possibly', comes the reply.
'Do I have to compromise, or can I be free...?'
I have had enough of justifying myself to a panel of
disbelievers,
of sinners, and of betrayers to the
Almighty forces of the Universe.

I am mocked by people who don't know anything
about that which they are judging.
They may slander me neglectful and foolish yet the
bitterness they stir in me represents their resistance
to a loving God.

My Lover

I canter forward to be near you
And create a space in time
The situation eases
Amongst the freedom that floats by
I am pulled under,
Pushed in the direction of a washed out moment
Overstepping the order and formality
Of a love kept in a photo album.
A reality meant for another
I betray the true love of my future
A crime in its sense
But right here we have a comfort that creates equilibrium,
A bridge that knows its boundaries
that delivers a strong support
We steal these special moments to satisfy our thirst
Eagerly awaiting an unmarked hail-stone
That may be thrown at us, in times apart.
But for now we seek refuge and engulf the love in our hearts.

A Song of Unrequited Love

A cavity of oneness
like a black whole of deception,
A pull into the unknown
is the trickery of seduction.
A questioning of honour?
A reality in time
I am swept into a cavity of oneness
without a border of time.

Like a flame in the morning
that motivates the day.
A radical shake up that
tried to give us away.

A cavity of oneness
A home in deceit
An honour in deception that leaves us weak.
A radical jump through a loophole in time
To be with you this moment leaves honour behind.
To bring light into the shadow is all that can be done.
There is truth and light in a heart of a soul
who sees past these weak areas and conquers his goals.

A love that is true, is beautiful and wise.
It holds hands and lights faces,
so all are elated!

The Devil Weighs no Gain

Devil blood red,
Back turned
Standing alone
His body wreathing through his gluttony filled belly of splendor,
Skin scaled like a dragon,
profiling gills with phlegm,
Long, poisoned tail,
Inked with a green crystalline sting
He knows his battle is fought
Lost to the miseries of the dark oceans
The game is over
I am triumphant
Deception and deceit
Revel away from me
Tenderly, I see a figure standing aloof, far off,
In a green field,
Bathing in the afternoon sun,
They are waiting for me.

I start to walk towards them out of the woods
At first, with the fear of my own vulnerability being

exposed
The true nature of my journey being seen in a glance.
I walk with pride
with full knowledge of whence I came
I know no limits to speak of.
The warmth of the sun
engulfs me
I relax and look back for a moment
Seeing the shadows amongst the trees,
The dewy floor beneath their boughs.
My feet relish the dry grass in which I stand
I allow myself to breath in the air and absorb the earth energy below my feet,
I am here now, arriving at the gateway to my destiny.

Blue Bird Flying in my Dreams

Dips to pick through Purple notches
Happy scenes
An anthropology of clutter,
A resistance
To a shutter!

Blessed sweet Angel
Spread thy wings
Surrender into the world,
Christen the days and find appropriate treasure, A life work
Beyond measure.

The Morals of An Angel

Give over to your desires
To will change in all that you perceive the world to need

Go into the future with an awareness of life beyond the mask
Go placidly, there is enough corruption in the midst of our daily chores
Rebel, but be true
We do not need to live by rule books
Integrity and true love are suffice.
Be kind,
Release anger, for its destructive
Do not allow confusion to rule you
Ground yourself in love and understanding
Give over to your urges only when you believe it does good
Speak and be spoken to
Do not let haste interfere with everyday accomplishments
Seek to find, to enjoy, to be happy and to infuse happiness.

To De-stress

Moon of night
Moon of light
As I move through the wondrous hours
Feel my flesh and limit me less
Release me from this darkening quest

Air, earth, fire and water ignite
I conquer up a quickening flight.
The air I ask to cleanse and banish,
The earth, bring love with each grounded step
Arousing the fertility of my breath.

Love shall hold me in a peaceful tire
baptising me through my hearts desire.
Soon I will arrive
To stand strong and elated
Enjoying my being by not being deflated

With courage I overcome the complexity of my
needs
I wander through the world without a sneeze.

Illusive Illusion

When searching for the point of truth in any situation
It is important to align yourself with your roots,
present and future reality.
Then look at your values, your needs and your
goals.
Take a deep breath and have a good look around.
You look up and there is your angel standing,
Close at hand.
One hand on your shoulder
and one on the phone,
waiting to connect a call,
Direct from God to confirm findings.
Challenges are easily over come as the years go by.
We keep on searching,
looking and finding,
then one day, in our lap arrives our reality.

The second half of our life,
the key to our future,
our home and our love.

All on a plate, ready to digest and share.
We align ourselves now in the direction of the future,

Ready to take off and rise up into a world
of evolving wonder.

Jealous Wisdom

Screaming, pacing through a dark alley way,

I am forced to confront an inner fear,
an inner rebellion,
A desire or need to be happy.
The happiness grows from my heart,
I watch others attempt to steal from their peers,
The light in me is something that gets stronger over time.
In those dark alley-ways,
I find the weak light within me,
within my own heart
revealing a way out of the madness
It is possible to be guided by the light,
following our hearts,
We enter into our dreams.

To all my Lovers, Male and Female

Today, I realised my friend couldn't truly 'see' me.
Strangely, as I turned my back, I saw you all, like a crowd,
Two score deep of soulful, beautiful people,
reaching out towards me,
Holding my heart.
How much you have given me as I pace through the darkness,
Sometimes scared and alone.
Suddenly for sure,
I know you have never and will never betray me.
Even if our lives cannot be together because of circumstance or dynamics,
I see you shining brightly
and know you will never let me down.
I love you all.

Wishing Well

Wishing well, wishing want
Wishing through the rise of time
Wanting well, wishing soon
We claim a space inside.

Deep, deep into the calm,
Late, late into the night.

Rising through the merry go round
Wanting, wishing, dreaming
Sliding, slipping, streaming
Dancing into a happiness,
Brushing through the foliage,
Tasting a moment,
Waking a song,
Listening to the morning cry,
The harp of a new day rising.

Wishing well, wishing want
Wishing through the rise of time
Wanting well, wishing soon
We claim a space inside
Deep, deep into the calm
Late, late into the night
Loving lost
Loving through
Wanting, rushing, rising,
Sliding, slipping, streaming

Dancing into a happiness,
Rising into a dream.
Hoping to find the moment is still rising.

Child in Darkness

When lost children grow up
They remain children inside

Encased in an adults body.
A part of them remains innocent and pure
Constantly searching for their play mate
To run free and share in elation.
As adults we look inside ourselves for purity and innocence
It remains preserved
Ready for a sacred moment;
A connection with another;
Innocent and pure.
An elated dance
Takes us up to the lightness of heaven
Shaking hands with Angels,
Singing songs of jubilation.
No longer in exile
We breath easily
Speak freely
And honour each other with joyous glances!

Hear My Call

I stood stagnant for hours
Unable to grasp the trickery
I was being subjected to
The fledgling I had become
had her wings clipped,
My screams of distress
sound shrill to the human ear.
So few can hear me for real
They need the reassurance of others
Unknowingly, they seek comfort from comrades
who hide their true status
Cowardice in the shadows of my unused power
Here we unveil the tale, because it is this action
which unites them in one overpowering goal.
The oppression continues,
Until one is so bold as to trust his very own heart
And unlock the door for me.

Loosing the game

A vestibule of choices,
A knife in the dark,
Slashing a glimpse,
Hacking a tone,
Waking a moment,
Loosing a dream,
Seeing it all dissolve In a pool of blood.
A sinking stone,
Dark and beyond.
Unknown to the future
The cause is out
The people in reign
Live to be true,
All hope must remain
Armageddon
Armageddon
Armageddon
We are fighting Armageddon
The Sacred, the Wise
The Mothers with their Child
The Damned, the Imprisoned
The oppressors of the millennium
We are fighting for our lives
STOP
Infinite wonder,
I see you here
The enlightened age is 'right here'
We seek to find
We seek to keep
We are the rulers
ALL THOSE THAT WEEP
Spend a moment
A space in time
GATHER IN LIGHT AND BE PREPARED TO
SHINE
The infinite wonder?
The holy ghost?
We are the damned,
the plagued,

the enlightened 'Rage'
Shake off the dust,
be prepared to stand.
We are the founders of our land.
A mass of voices raised to the sky
To conquer and bring
Salvation to our inner king.
Give into your soul,
Remember your zone
Your heart is alive and ready to act
My crown is replenished and fully fed
Truth, Love and Fairness,
CONQUER THAT.

In Gentlemen's Favour

Upstanding gentlemen
Dim in the limelight
At ease with themselves
As their hearts miss a cord.
A thorough fair of movement
A city of nights
Dark in the shadows
They were born to fight.
Watching the back stabbing,
I tremble, scared and withdrawn.
The towers of democracy,
Quiver
Waiting to fall.
Out of the ashes
There is hope in the light
Guided by Gentlemen
Who don't want to give up their fight.
A land of plenty
Conquers lack in our hands
Giving out hand outs
When Truth leaves their plans.
A prison filled with Gentlemen
All benefit frauds

A land of plenty
Guided by cause.
The human position
Is frank and corrupt
When order and love reign
We will become democrats.

Fool's Gold

Rivers running through the flow of life
Can often lead to a place of magic,
A place of destiny,
A place to unearth the sorrows of mankind.
Diving down to the bottom of the river bed
I am filled with want as I see flickers of gold. The
sand clears and the gold dissolves into light
Shocked and disappointed in my risk taking,
I feel foolish,
Choking,
I struggle to the surface,
I realise the light is more beautiful
And more powerful than any golden nugget.
I find my destiny in these moments.
The more I embrace light,
The more the path of my destiny becomes paved
with gold.

Seeing Through

Water runs down into a spiral abyss of darkness
The water transforms into hope and glory amongst
the chaos of life.
We do not need such a hope in this area
I am to go beyond the grave one more time.
To live in two worlds is truly magical
It is open to all of us,

The world is so much more fantastic than I could
ever have dreamed;
I did not know,
for so many years,
I appeared to be in darkness,
I could not see through the night,
One step at a time.

Dew

When the first drop of dew hits the ground,
It smashes into a thousand fragments of colour,
Each with their own consciousness,
Their own life and the ability to evolve creativity,
Into the timely space of eternity.

Broken Arrow

I was chasing an arrow through the woods and
stumbled across a deserted moment,
It was a remembrance of a past feeling,
A desire.
Encapsulated and lost,
I blindly moved forward only to be reminded of my
limitations,
Chasing through the depths of my heart I came to a
lay-by where there was a sea urchin perspiring.
Reaching out I was stung by an impeccable desire
To win back the object of my raging heart.
It was not a case of want,
It was a magical moment,
Based on integrity.
It was a need to win back my eternal love.
None has been such a greater desire,
How lost I have been in these moments.
I know what it is to loose,
To win is my conquest.

Piccadilly Circus

Flashing lights
Smiling skies
Mortal chaos
Cryptic highs.
I am in a crowd of alliance,
Shy in the background,
seeking a connection
Darting a glance
Filling my desires
With a small outburst.

Stepping through the shadows;
A lightning interplay,
Forwards and backward,
A spark in the dark.
A ruffle on occasion
Administering a rebuke,
Forwards and backwards,
A link to the park.
Waltzing around
I sniff an odor of revenge
Sideways and backwards
It's hard to seek amendment.
Another half
Lost in the park
I aim for pursuit.
Forwards and backwards
Light and dark.
Looking for that person
Another minute goes by.
Watching and waiting
I am on a high
A challenge to be near her
And take centre stage.
Watching and waiting
Time seems to slowly pass by
The thoughts that are with me saunter around
Questioning my intentions
and a need to have my feet on the ground.

I feel alive
I wonder if I am being real
A thought of past deception
A need for respite
A link into the future
That brings second sight
A given moment
Sprung from time.

I am caught unawares
As she presents in time.

A justified motion
No need for regret
A killer look of opportunity
As we hasten to come forward,
from deep back.
Stealing a glance
Wanting an eye
Feeling a connection
We venture into second vision.
Deep set and comfortable
We are onto second base,
Looking for security
In the way we are placed.
A warrant for exposure
A need for truth
Laughing and joking,
We perform our credentials.
Unaware and preoccupied
We head for the coast
Wondering if its possible,
To throw out a rope;
Tying the moment
Knotting the occasion
Wrapping the gift
Objectifying a will
Through a myriad of emotion.
A quickening pace

A circular movement
A want to dance
and set the wheels in motion,
A recognition of a life
With no regrets
I am on a high
I trust in this cause
Slowly I breath
Quickly I respond
I know there is truth
in all I am feeling.
To be met by this person
Is not to be sniffed at
It seems like an equation
That holds a card,
A rooted ambition
A destiny in motion
That lights my fire
And holds a horizon
filled with thirst quenched skies.
Our hands clasp
Grabbing at the equation
Knowing it works

'Do you like Jazz?'
We enter into the park.

Can you Hear me Sweetheart

Lets be together before the day is out
I was thinking about you in the night
Your finger tips were near yet your heart was far,
I felt like you had travelled and it wasn't in the car.
In my dreams, I saw a meeting of angels
'What was said? Do they have plans?'
The ladies of the night are many,
They laid out a good spread,
Quelling desires to be with you,
Archangel Michael whispered sweetly,

'I asked for such advice?'
As I found myself set off into the depth of the
cushioning of a feathered embrace
Of a goose feathered duvet,
Ha, nothing more.

Through a Questioning of Worth

I spin to confront you
And examine you
You point the finger
And allocate the crime
I give over
And give regard,
A fundamental retort:

A wish to be more than
To sink deeper than
To live more truthfully than
To scream more positively than
To love more wholesomely than
Because
There is nothing more.
My head bows,
You turn your back,
We feel discomfort
We know that.
We wish for choices,
And see a crisis,
A desolation of systematic evolution;
A worth that amounts,
To the greater part
Of having it all
And living with an open heart.
We look at each other,
Deep into the soul,
Confronting our fears,
We know we seek pleasure
In our hearts,

To be free,
A wish for a future
It is a dream
To run free.

Integrated and Whole

Surrounded by my inevitability
I look deep within you
Seeking to move past the mask of incompleteness
That captures this empty moment,
Falling into a void of space,
I am launched into another dimension.
Integrated and whole,
I float through a cavity,
A cavity of oneness,
An everlasting dimension that is plentiful and light,
A cavity of oneness, integrated and whole.
A flight into fortune
That came unstuck at the seams
A launch into space with a gathering pace
A walk in the dark that became
A flight into the light,
Hope has now left me
As I have second sight.

I am Lost in a Waking Dream

Turning around
I see you standing there,
The light blinds me
As I enwrap myself in the emotions of my heart,
Wanting to be bathed in a warm beautiful light
That wills a new beginning
and warrants a holding,
A closeness that connects and holds our souls.
I feel the strength of your presence

And am willed to exchange an energetic love
With this life changing encounter,
I want to be fully present and remain in this dream,
As I wake and turn to hold you.

To Blossom with Pink Blush

My heart yearns to be touched.
To reach out to the spirit of destiny and be
vanquished to a place of love and life,
I can applaud all those that have found true love.
Please spare a moment for those that have to
endure the moments, questioning their faults,
gaining self-acceptance and inner peace to be able
to be accepted by a wider audience.
If there is a fickle thing in life,
It is the superficiality of our relationships,
Connections seem sometimes to only pass us by for
a moment,
then they are dashed on the rocks,
Not only because of deceit or betrayal

Often because of inner love,
Often because of a deeper understanding.

We see deeply into our soul mates eyes and feel
that we have seen them before.
We celebrate,
However, as soon as our interests change,
Instead of celebrating this new found freedom
Our comrade goes into a state of anxious chaos,
An unanchored emotional revolt,
of loss, power and dignity.
In our being we hold nothing short of an added
interest in life.
I laugh and ridicule the superficiality of such
exchanges,
Of such temporary moments with another soul.

Growth matters, growth should be given space to breath and be shared,
However it is the most threatening part of a relationship.

A Sailor's Pace

We lost our grace,
Got stuck in the chase,
Derailed,
without a saving grace,
Yet the rising of pain brought as back to a place,
In which the chaos and the angst took second place.

In which the sun shines down,
To ignite a warmth,
That makes all this carnage
Seem like a reason to abort.

Through the light of day,
If destiny departs,
we have no chance in our hearts.
Yet the sense of time keeps ticking on,
with a knowledge that true hearts speak on.

With truth in mind there is a grace which saves,
From all who enter in to her waves,
A faith in all that brings peace and light,
that illuminates simply by shinning a light!

A flood of juices runs deep into the night,
pulling down in to the ocean without any fight.

The sense of freedom that can be seen right here,
Is a surrendering to living without any fear.

A touch so deep that casts out the night and brings grace to those who want live without fight.

A beauty in seasons that allows truth to steer and
gives opportunity when once there was fear.

A ship of union that sails through the night and
arrives at safe waters to ground and ignite!

Although the tale casts a twist as the adventure
begins,

You find yourself a sailor taken by the wind.
I arrive at land,
Feet sturdy and sure,
As you head off in to the waves for more,

Casting a net as deep as the day,
To enable a repeat of a mermaids interplay,
As they find themselves on deck,
singing their songs with many chords,
They become unversed in the models of accord,

Diving for courage their journey continues,
As they find their rebellion and continue their cause.

A true sailor at heart,
The tale has no ending
As the conclusion hasn't embarked,
An opportunity for adventure,
He keeps a strong heart.

The stars shine down o give destiny a chance,
Catalysing choice as they register lonely hearts,

Stars that shine to give light to all,
To take care of burdens and illuminate pain,
A call through the ages that governs through choice,

Yet is inspired by purpose and following one's call!

And here lies the magic,
For to 'follow one's call' gives reason and purpose to
life's hurdles and falls.

Giving grace an understanding,
As she acts full beam in the night,
giving direction and respite to all,
Who enter into their second sight!

One Moment

My head turned to stare
Into the centre of the sinking sun,
Absorbing the warmth of its full intensity.
I am held me for a moment whilst I integrate my
recent learning.
Shame and confusion enwrapped me,
whilst I try to get to grips
with the horror
of the dialogue
that was spoken moments before.
We can feel so distant from our partner,
yet we are united in a common goal of wanting love
and happiness.
Sometimes that bridge between two people seems
such a long path to cross,
Sometimes it isn't possible to meet in the middle. I
start the approach
and find myself freestanding,

Alone and without pity,
Mainly because of a black hole;
A lack of understanding
in the troubles of humanity.

We read and weep,
We gain and loose
but above all we need to be there;
Present, listening and absorbing, connecting the
missing parts,
Networking a path into the future
that connects us all with happiness and love.

The march is forthright, standing shoulder to shoulder.
Together our paths bond to create ample soul food for all,
Extending a web for others to interweave their desires and searches, Into a reality of heartfelt happiness.

Walking Tall

Enduring the heady flashes of pain I walk freely,
Standing tall,
With reassurance that I am myself,
In my strength,
In my innocence,
In my freedom.
You have a want for me to live as an exploited teenager,
This is a call from beyond
To assert a will into compromise,
To flatten my assets and clip my rights,
To become less of myself,
Without value
But with endurance
As I am abducted from the most graceful place of contentment.
Walking on air
I acknowledge our connection,
Less spiritual,
More emotional,
Physical
A heart in the mind and the soul
That brings a journey into corruption.
I acknowledge everything that it is
Yet I know it's you who has chosen this path,
I am just a bystander,
Walking with you for a brief moment
Through your shadows,
With an open heart.

Sometimes, staying open on this journey has been hard,
I have worked to earn through my own rights,
A lightness and a happiness,
To be dragged into a position that shows traits of my past has been uncomfortable,
Painful
It reminds me of everything I have been through and been trapped in,
Yet there has been even more learning from this position.
I am looking at being free now,
to walk forward,
To enjoy lightness,
love and expansive living,
To live in a limitless and infinite reality,
More attuned to the enlightened state of my earning
This honour I need reflected in my love,
In divinity
In sacredness
In being connected to the grand master,
As I work with the consciousness and energy of Creation;
Feeling the power seep through me,
touching all in my path
Whom have a will to experience their own magnificence.
Humour me in my beauty
Laugh at what seems to be my ego
My work is done
You see everything in its complexity
I have released myself from your games and given you the option of lightness.
This is your attraction to me
A calling from within you,
That you will find hard to acknowledge in its consciousness.
It is this one realisation you wanted confirmation from me in your achievement,
Feel free to make your choices,
To decide on your next turn,

And to allow yourself time to arrive at a destination
of true peace,
Or continue in a compromised state of being
living in fear of the complexities of love.
Your life is your responsibility,
Take care my love.

Star Gazing on Secrets

As the rivers reflect the starry skies,
I turn my gaze in to the deep,
Seeking solitude in a wealth of experience that
leaves no stone unturned,
No life in slow motion.
The emotive waters wash through the soul,
To heal those still standing on the battlefield,
The warriors abandon their stand,
They are exposed as trust is lost to valour,
Courage to a dependable heart,
In which the light and love of a future in its simplicity
Washes away from delivering unhindered results.
These are the turning tides of the sky as the stars
shine on the waters of temptation.

A yearning for desired results without the generosity
of heartfelt love.
To sink deeper in to the wounds of soiled love,
is to bath one's skin with ointment and salts,
with a healing balm and chequered innocence.
The informative years of hurt and pain dominate an
open scenery,
Of creative magic that allows the aesthetics of a
new era to replant its seeds and nourish its roots.

The stars tell the true nature of the story,
to all whom gaze upon them.
Guiding a new path and a new awakening of heart.

Venus over Ben Nevis

Whilst watching the falling stars
We ponder over our dreams
Catching a falling star maybe seen as a sin
Or is it the Master plan?
The gaze of millions draws near in the quest of the light of Orion
Yet caught up in their futile passions
We wish for silence and stillness.
Until the roar of Mother Gaia
Conquers through the strata
Quenching a longing for compassion,
Wholesomeness and a presence.
Oh, to be naked within.

Casting Effect

The tide stirs an awakening
Far a field,
Saturn's golden light reaches in to the emptiness of a heart in the wake of desire,
Stirring a myriad of emotional cries,
Restless in the gaze of wondering eyes and far fetched dreams.
Waking from the chide of a slow rising sun
Competing for the attention in the night
Destined to bring waves of want and prosperity yet belittled by a closer pale and wanton bride
Venus casts her light shadow,
Sparking a catalyst of chaos as man struggles to order his dreams and prioritise his motions.
This is a planetary task.
Gazing down the path of destiny,
in the questioning of desire and in the manifestation of dreams.
Seek not to stir in to the gaze,
As stone may embody you.
Ashes to ashes

Allow the rebirth of your destiny
To be born of thyself and evolved beyond your
eternal being.
Peace is with thy as you seek,
To dig heals in to the moment of chastised heart
Breathing slowly to allow the warmth of an inner sun
Is to illuminate and align golden fingers of light in to
the fields of destiny.
A magnitude of experience sought out and validated
through the university of time,
Eternity and the simple breath of your being.
Be still my sweet.

Breathing in Light

Darts of inspiration
Spark moments of pleasure
In a turmoil of pain that could of led to a drowning;
Harmoniously arranged scales of new colors
Leap forward
To find of flow of encouragement
and swallow the will to live freely
In the womb of compassion.
Creating life abound with futuristic hopes and
enlightened thinking suited not only for the
innocence and young but the elders and the wise.

Red Handkerchief

Red handkerchieves wave in the mid day sun
Opening up the blister of my heart
A warning to remember the good times,
To be in a life of dark moments that seize and
paralyse us from our daily routines
Is a choice I have come to reject.
There is a definitive warning that comes with this
vision,

Create a beautiful life filled with
happiness, love and peace.

Black Lobster

A Black lobster strides my heart space,
Intoxicating my soul
With a want to extinguish me
From my potential interests.
His desires are futile,
His passion longing,
An empty projection
Designed to intoxicate
and damage a clear thinking heart.
Archangel Michael loosens the lobster's grip,
To breath pink and red tones into the creature's shell.
The lobster, astounded by the brightness of the light,
Directs his gaze longingly out towards the glistening ocean,
Michael looks concerned at the lack of love the creatures holds,
In the dry air it neither poisons nor lives,
He questions whether to give the lobster its freedom in the ocean?
This creature is ready for a new awareness,
To be enlightened in to the spiritual world of eternal existence.
Hence, it has no place or purpose,
He becomes an entity ready for evolution,
Released of its toxicity
Yet impotent to its own power.
A crayfish ready to work itself up the ladder,
of kindness, love and light.

A World Full of Fools

In a world full of choices,
A freedom over the land
The white horses gather,
To sweep us up into the reaches of a hand
Spinning into the now
I turn and arrive,
I wish upon this moment
To look deep into your eyes.
Seeing past a concrete thorough fair
I am moved to became
A credit to society
Because I look into the mirror
At the fool that I have become.
We are all warriors of an illusion
A game of power
A play on words
That lights our fires and sings to our desires.
I am motivated to laugh
As I am carried home
By a horse, of course!

In the Light of Darkness

Anger and frustration enwrap me
As I look into the eyes of a perpetrator
and wonder what it is that makes her feel her value,
Makes her see me in a light of darkness.
In fact,
I question those that judge me on a daily basis.
Those that see me happy and free
but have no idea of my past suffering.
It is wonderful to be happy and to know that I am
free but the unexpected shock that meets me in this
place is the resentment and judgment from the
unhappy people that surround me.

Judging me on a scale of their own daily pain.
Unable to see that my joy has been a gift of healing,
a work with Creation;
One that I share and more than that,
am happy to give to all.
I am met with so much envy and jealousy,
I wonder if it is possible to stay on this plane,
I know that I must ground and trust and give a kind glance
But I would have it known that 80%
of the people sitting around this table cannot meet me with a positive glance,
Embrace the light of opportunity!

Pushed On

An evergreen adventure,
A candy floss sky,
A leap into space,
With a cry!
Above a pimpernel array of crimes,
Leaping over a crevice
At a shooting pace.
An adventure into a dream
Across a bridge of sorrow
A-wake in the morning,
A walk in the dark,
A flight of fantasy,
It's a cruel spark,
Feeling abandoned,
I let out a cry
'Peace to my people,
Don't let me die'
Give me grace and favour
To liberate the light,
So we may sing and come hither to win our fight!

Humour Me

Bizarre intuitive activity leads to an accurate sense
of awareness,
An inner truth,
And a love of a fantastic Angel
Who is able to leap into existence
Through a mindful calling.

The Flame on the Hill

The waking flag of humble pie
The deli of choice in a land of rich soil,
We are singed with heat,
To wither and coil.
The loins of mens desires
Cause them to bury their heads
And conquer a spread,
That sparks a ring of fire,
Flaring down into the gasping crowd
Tongues are blazing,
The breaking wind
Captivates the morning,
As the flames spread.

Blushing with Desire

Compatible to a rose bush
with thorns seeping into a shadow
of blood filled adventures
Be careful my sweet
A poisoned chalice is a life time of regrets,
refurbished into a dreamland of emptiness.

I wish for you that in every moment you will
understand love

and become near to the joyous moments that dwell inside you.

I choose a life filled with love, joy and a sweetened sense of desire with a truth quenched so close to the bone it leaves me gasping for breath.

I see my loved one holding a dew drop
so delicately balanced, all is said for eternity.
Its not you my love, but I wish you well.
Slipping Through
The twelfth hour arrives and I am reborn into a moment in destiny that I forgot to arrange.

I seem to have forgotten to plan this part,
As I am sitting alone and destitute.
Aware that there is so much I could do
Yet I am burdened by the emptiness of my futile passions.

An angel is coming to see me,
To uplift me and help me understand that there is more coming to me,
I must be patient.
I did not realise how soul destroying it can be to be human,

The limitations of emotions,
Society and physicality are debilitating.
The stupidity of politics,
of lust and greed,
just add to a 'human's' despair.

The circle of life expresses itself in an hour-glass of sand.
Soon, all will be dissolved and it will be hard to know if existence is possible.
Such is the weakness of my heart.

TIC TAC

Tic Tac
Jump Jack
Sin City
Out back
Tin man, hope plan,
Maintain your gain.

Smiling faces,
Caught out races.
Arriving at a destination,
Yellow signs
Bowed out stations
Flapping ribbons,
Saddened races,
Bloody causes
Hacked out faces
No life in the places.

Tic Tac
Jump Jack
Sin City
Out back
Tin man, hope plan
Maintain your gain.

Go for your dreams
Don't take second best
It's a crippled society
In a shadow of regret,
You bring awareness,
of truth and light;
Be here tomorrow,
Stand in your cause,
Put the word out,
'Refrain from the pain'
'It's a loosing reign'

Tic Tac
Jump Jack

Sin City
Out back
Tin man, hope plan
Maintain your gain.
Survive the 'Reign',
Be a King,
Solomon's in
Tired faces
Burnt out places
Still remain.
Be wise,
be Cool
Solomon is in
'Refrain from the pain,
It's a loosing reign'.
Tin man, hope plan
Tired Races
Life in dark places
Smiling faces
Caught out races
Hearty places
Maintain your gain
'Your dreams remain'.

Look at the light
See the colour
Feel the joy
An apocalypse of laughter
Will remain.

A life for living
With no regret
Don't take second best
Your dreams are worthy,
They are the cause,
They are the light,
And the soul,
worth being hearty for.

Tin man, hope plan

Tired Races
Life in dark places
Smiling faces
Caught out races
Hearty places

Maintain your gain
Your dreams remain.
Go for your dreams
Don't take second best
It's a crippled society
In a shadow of regret

You bring awareness
A truth and light
Stand for your dreams
Listen to your choices,
A vestibule of voices.

Tin man, hope plan
Tired Races
Life in dark places
Smiling faces
Caught out races
Hearty places
Maintain your gain
Your dreams remain.

Guarded secrets,
Locked out weakness.
All hope remains

Stay true to the field
Know the cause
Shoot your desires
For a fairer scene.

Tin man, hope plan
Tired Races
Life in dark places
Smiling faces

Caught out races
Hearty places,
Maintain your gain.

A constant inter-change
A striking moment
All power remains
Your head is strong
Your needs are clear
The dream is out,
don't let anything interfere.

Tin man, hope plan
Tired Races
Life in dark places
Smiling faces
Caught out races
Hearty places
Maintain your gain
'YOUR DREAMS DO REMAIN'

A World of Fools

The fool in the mirror
Awakens to the day
I wish to be here
And to realise my ways
I look at the city
The techno warrior I have become,
Armed with a gold credit card
Black lace and a thong,
I stride down the platform
Launch into the city
Then deviate to the bus shelter
Where I speak easy, help quickly;
I want to be real, its what I am about.
My philosophy is vast
But what can I show?
My pockets are empty

My card is plastic,
The bank account is in debit,
It's an illusion on paper
A form of deceit.
I wish to be real now
To be seen now
To live now
To change now
To arrive now;
In a place that honours this moment
And sees gold all around,
That stops buying into the illusions of marketing scams
And respects destiny
Amongst the gloss of indulgence;
With a cavalry of choices.

Death through a 'Walk Out'

Choosing a telecom personality Is an offering to the Gods
To crucify one's life
and give out one last gulp.
Distinguished for a moment
The shadows enter in
As the soul sees shame and sorrow;
A life in tatters;
The truth still remains.
Mothers and daughters
Abandoned and accused;
The expectations of living are hard to resolve.

Pebbles speak loudly
Cursing the times
Skimming over grace and favour,
And those left behind.

An offering of an angel gives second birth;
Into a life of choices

With hope and freedom,
A chance for new birth.

('Walk in' or ''Walk out' are terms used when a person exchanges their soul for another's in one body)

Loving Breeze

Hearing the sound of the trees,
Wind rushes through me,
Rustling up through the avenue,
I rise to be amongst them, brushing my soul through their feathered fingers,
Higher, to the green tips.
The trees reach up to heaven,
Their energy fresh
And full of new of life
The delicacy of their leaves is like the softness of new born skin,
Vulnerable and vivid,
As if straight from God's hands
Like a gift from heaven itself,
Amongst the trees I feel held in a womb of love.
I go up to heaven to thank God himself and master at his Creation.

Where are We?

We are on a pivot of opportunities
A rising star
A sinking sun
A homeland to dwell
To romance and become.
A thorough fair of movement
A city of life
A light in my head
That warrants a trend

A rendezvous in the moment
A whisper of exchanges
A need for peace
A tender release.
An eye cast to the shadows
A flicker to the light
A spark of defiance as we enter into second sight!

Divine Love

The heart and soul suck the seeds of
disappointment
As they copulate in serenity.
Live for love, for dreams,
For the present and until the end of time.
Forgive me for my dreams,
Lust in the eternal
And love
Satisfies the temperature of my confusion.
I am not afraid of tomorrow, as I should be, or as it
is a will for me to be,
Death's mask has been lifted,
Death is my friend.
I speak only the truth,
With a will to be certain,
To be whole and to continue to remain in the
present
Without boundaries of the past
or lack of knowledge in the moment.
Anger has no place in my body or soul,
I ask that it be dismissed.
Halo and be with me,
Stand with me,
Face the morrow with me,
Stand at the top of the mountain
And allow yourself to be swept through the valleys
to the earth,
To compete with the rain and the thunder.
To be triumphant over the lightning and the

tornados.
I ask this for the sake of the present and the future.

Starlight Beauty

Beauty is the mirror of innocence of which you have sprung,
Deep in the universe there is a star which manifests many dreams.
Those dreams spring up in their numbers
And wipe through childish reflections,
They have the power to transport you through the stars.
Keep the innocence of your dreams alive and you will own the Stars.

A Life in the Wings

A life in the wings
A destiny of sorts
A need for appeasement
Through a score of remorse

A hapless warrior
A ritualistic touch
A ceremony in motion
That leaves questions unanswered.

A want for a finale
A hope for a future
A life in rewind
Past a tyranny in taut

A hapless warrior
A ritualistic touch
A ceremony in motion
That leaves questions unanswered.

Count through the moments
Speak through the days
Give over to enrolling
Its a matter of days.

A hapless warrior
A ritualistic touch
A ceremony in motion
That leaves questions unanswered.

A victory in time
An upheaval in cause
I am left with a tyranny in motion
And no sense of discourse.
Peace will be mine.

Third Party Love

Hence how we watch the day unfold,
Unjust and ready for the changing tide.

Unfairly we kiss the morning dew and seek pleasure
in our ways,
Capitalised with a sense of loss
Regret and confusion in our united presence,
As we shake with the earth in bitter sorrow,
At such an unjust freedom.
The tides change,
The sorrow breeds,
An alliance with an arrow.

I ask him to forgive me in this space of unforgiving
heart,
Breathing in death,
as the futility
Enters its final stage,
Standing tall in his presence,
Life flows through me,
Giving grace and favour,

With a message in a kiss.

The song on the horizon sings a tune;
A light cry in the midst of the dawning day,
Cherished but without a prayer.
Blessed be the,
in thy way my love, see hither.

Sing to me in tune
You leave unanswered prose,
I give gratitude towards the turning tide,
We speak to deliver by following through,
And now give thanks to our destiny and chosen psalm.
A moments prayer, as the hovering dew enters its final stage of presence and draws an earthly moment of activity in an embrace.

A breath is all that remains as he walks away, to another's arms,
And the dew dissolves in a timely manner,
As the warm sun of 'emptiness' blesses me.

The Importance of Feeding the Heart

Living with deception is a symbol of love unreceived;
The heart is in debt.
Abundance of love is feeling secure in heart consciousness,
That one has a mass of love to give,
And there is plenty around to receive.
The heart steps back in the flow of love energy
by receiving nourishment and acceptance through the self, others and source.
Live for love

The Magnetic Poles of Choice

Strange powers possess the weak hearted
When they claim their stake
Amongst a chaos of overriding arcadia
This action does seem to dazzle people in the street
We wish not to burden such a structure of truth
As it sits placid amongst the dust
Not interchanging its wishes
But finding accordance with the days polarities
We look in to the eyes of deceit and yet are met with
a vision of a catastrophic ending.

I was a prisoner to myself for years
Yet breathing deeply I reformed and created a chain
of words in truth.
This I wish for you in lightness and simplicity.

Nourishing a Heart

A shinning heart lights up the darkest shadow,
Bringing love to the deepest pit of neglect and
sorrow in another,
Forming a pathway into an experience of divine truth
and unity.
I will take your hand and walk you through the shady
glen
To enter in to the lightness and warmth of an all
seeing sou
Wise beyond his human years.
You will feel the core strength and warmth of deep
understanding
As to replenish your beauty within,
So you may blossom and unfold into your truc
natural magnificence.

Non Spaces

Rose curtains stand tall through deep corridors,
Carpets with corners lock up the night
Whilst they undress you, out of sight.
They move through the passageway
In to the limelight,
No point complaining,
We are all gaining
As we step up in to the light.
I am living in a dream that collides
With the passageways of time,
A temperamental exchange,
A meeting of minds,
As we wander up through the stairwell,
In to 'Starlight'.

Eclipse of the Heart

Twilight is the colour of my despair,
As I look in to the moon,
The lightness of Shadow
Beams through my heart,
To vanquish my soul
From the destitution of my desires.

Speak to me in Tongues

The answers in life are kept in a book beyond the Stars,
Although a paralysis of words seeps through me in this confused moment;
I am heard without rhapsody.
Speak out to me for I am lost and without ears,
Only the touch of your love will stir my muscles to react,
The paralysis of my tongue engulfs me.

I tried to look past the hour glass
And was met with a pensive attack towards the future architecture of my life,
In my stare I was not heard,
for fear took root and sank me in to the stone in which I had leapt moments before.
This is not my truth,
It is my destiny.
Do you understand?
I had no control over myself in this moment.
When I fight to survive,
I am motivated in hope towards a life with freedom,
Physical paralysis is that which I run free from
But I find myself trapped in a future of which the world has no resources to support my aims.
I go about my work to set others free
And hope that I maybe free one day
To speak with a loose tongue,
This is my uncontrollable desire to survive,
Written in the book beyond the Stars,
I find my destiny and my fate.

Spring

A bendy moment
Presents through a concubine of uncertainty
Damaging a life in overview
When we look in to reflective waters
The decaying leaves of autumn bring change,
As they are swept away and spring flowers fight through.

Together Again

I reach out to your finger tips

Clasping our hands
I draw a deep breath
Our eyes meet
Looking into our souls
We move our bodies closer
pressing,
holding,
clasping.
I feel the softness of your lips
Brushing against my cheeks
Searching for an intimate connection
The missing part
I turn to look at you
Our lips seal the exchange
Motivating the moment
Peeling back the layers
Closer and brighter
The temperature rises
Looking upwards and onwards
Rising up in ecstasy
The energy exchanges
Builds faster
Happier, Deeper
My hands search for the place inside
That holds your tenderness,
That place in you that is real
Whole and wanted
Finding that missing part
I burst through your physical body
Becoming expansive generous, light and giving,
Knowledgeable and infinite
At this point I am seeking the advice of the Angels
Home again
I look for another way to embrace,
Another magnified dream.
The light blinds me,
As I become integrated in the oneness,
The Godliness,
The sacredness of ecstasy.
The ultimate light is savoured
Adorned and captured.

I question you, your own experience?
And am met with a strange response.
I leave with me, my own journey.
Infinite and life giving,
But this was for me only.
I was taken to the highest pitch of light and met with
the company of heaven.
My fellow men.
How strange is the wonder of life.

Rebirth

Today I stumbled upon the core of my pain,
An egg waiting for the hatching,
Chipping away at circumstance,
searching for a renewed sense of spirit.
I was driven yet deeper into the portals of clearing,
Searching through the universe inside myself,
to gain back my generosity of spirit,
In living, loving and finding desire for the passion of
life.

Opening the Heart's Aquarium into a River of Love

Little goldfish nibble away at the oxygen in my heart,
Feeding their bellies with glistening enthusiasm and
inspiration for the day;
The lily pads lie still,
As their flowers open up,
Aching to be touched,
Stroked and painted.
Their roots shoot down in to the murky waters
beneath
Hidden to the onlookers gaze.
The illusion of shadow in spirit,
Surpasses the glorious and divine,

beauty seen on the surface.
Enlightened souls
See only beauty without shade or shadow.
Abundant in light and love there is no need to look into the shadows,
The enlightened heart is blind,
Glorious and sublime we bathe in abundant heart
So as to create a clear channel,
That spills over the banks
Into a river with a thick flow,
There is plenty of nourishment here,
The big fish as well as the little fish,
Feed off the oxygen.

The Enchanted Void

In the forest of imagination,
As nymphs in the night,
We allow the passing of time,
I had a flash back to a waking tide.

Feeling the isolation and emptiness of a disconnection to all that was.
I found myself in a tunnel,
Feeling as an object looking in to the mirror,
Of a well without end,
A void that without soul,
The experience left me to fall into infinite darkness,
Hastily, I embraced my soul and found my salvation and my peace.
Building and constructing my life by embracing all things living and giving of life.
Through a passing of time and a passage of choice,
I found internal growth,
Through all things beautiful and natural.
I was awakened and enlightened,
Into a state of ecstasy,
Light and love.
As I step forward on the journey in the present day,

I know to, touch all, bringing people to magical state
of contentment.
I to, give life and nourishment to those whom are
lost and trapped, in a sense of emotive confusion.
Life gives life,
life gives happiness,
nourishment, beauty and love.
To embrace life is to feed one's soul.

Stand True

Life is enduring
Its a matter of course
To see in to the future
Is a curse and a cause
Light hearted and open
We need a break
To reduce all our fears
In a way that isn't weak
Or makes us geeks.
Life beyond death
Is a miracle of sorts
But the truth that surrounds us
Is just waiting for science to take its course.

Seeds of Light, was written as a journal of poetic personal experience, in the ups and downs of relationships and life.

Amanda uses writing as a tool for transformation towards peace and lightness. Amanda works creatively with universal consciousness, she supports creative integrity within the arts. Amanda works to aid personal development, wellness, creative expression and with 'communications' by channeling from a place of divine inspiration and vision.

A consultation with Amanda is an enlightening experience that brings transformation on many levels. Amanda comes from a creative background, originally visual art. Over time, she has found her writing and vocal channels have opened up. She integrates universal consciousness with creativity and 'communications', reaching people from all creative, cultural and spiritual areas of life.

www.belovedlight.com

For Development and Communications
'A Life of Bliss' by Amanda McGregor

Made in the USA
Charleston, SC
18 May 2016